Lineberger Memorial
Library
Lutheran Theological Southern Seminary Columbia, S. C.

The Lord's Prayer

Illustrated by

Tim Ladwig

Eerdmans Books for Young Readers
Grand Rapids, Michigan / Cambridge, U.K.

Published 2000 by Eerdmans Books for Young Readers
An imprint of Wm. B. Eerdmans Publishing Company
255 Jefferson S.E., Grand Rapids, Michigan 49503
P.O. Box 163, Cambridge CB39PU U.K.

Printed in Hong Kong

00 01 02 03 04 05 6 5 4 3 2 1

Library of Congress Cataloging-in-Publication Data
Ladwig, Tim
The Lord's Prayer / illustrated by Tim Ladwig
p. cm.
ISBN 0-8028-5180-0 (alk. paper)
1. Lord's prayer Juvenile literature.
2. Afro American children Prayer books
and devotions English.
I. Title
BV232.L23 1999
226.9'609505 dc21 98 52477
CIP
AC

The paintings were done with watercolor
using glazing technique on 140 pound
Arches cold press watercolor paper.
Pastels and fluid acrylics were used
over the watercolor.

The text was set in Stone Informal.
The book was designed by Gayle Brown.

To Don Davis
and in memory of his father, Mr. Ted Davis.
They have both taught us who our Father is.
—T. L.

Our Father in heaven,

hallowed be your name.

TED DAVIS
EXTERIOR REPAIR • LAWN CARE • PAINTING

MBER & SUPPLY

DELI

Your kingdom come.

Your will be done

on earth as it is in heaven.

Papas
DELI

Give us this day our daily bread.

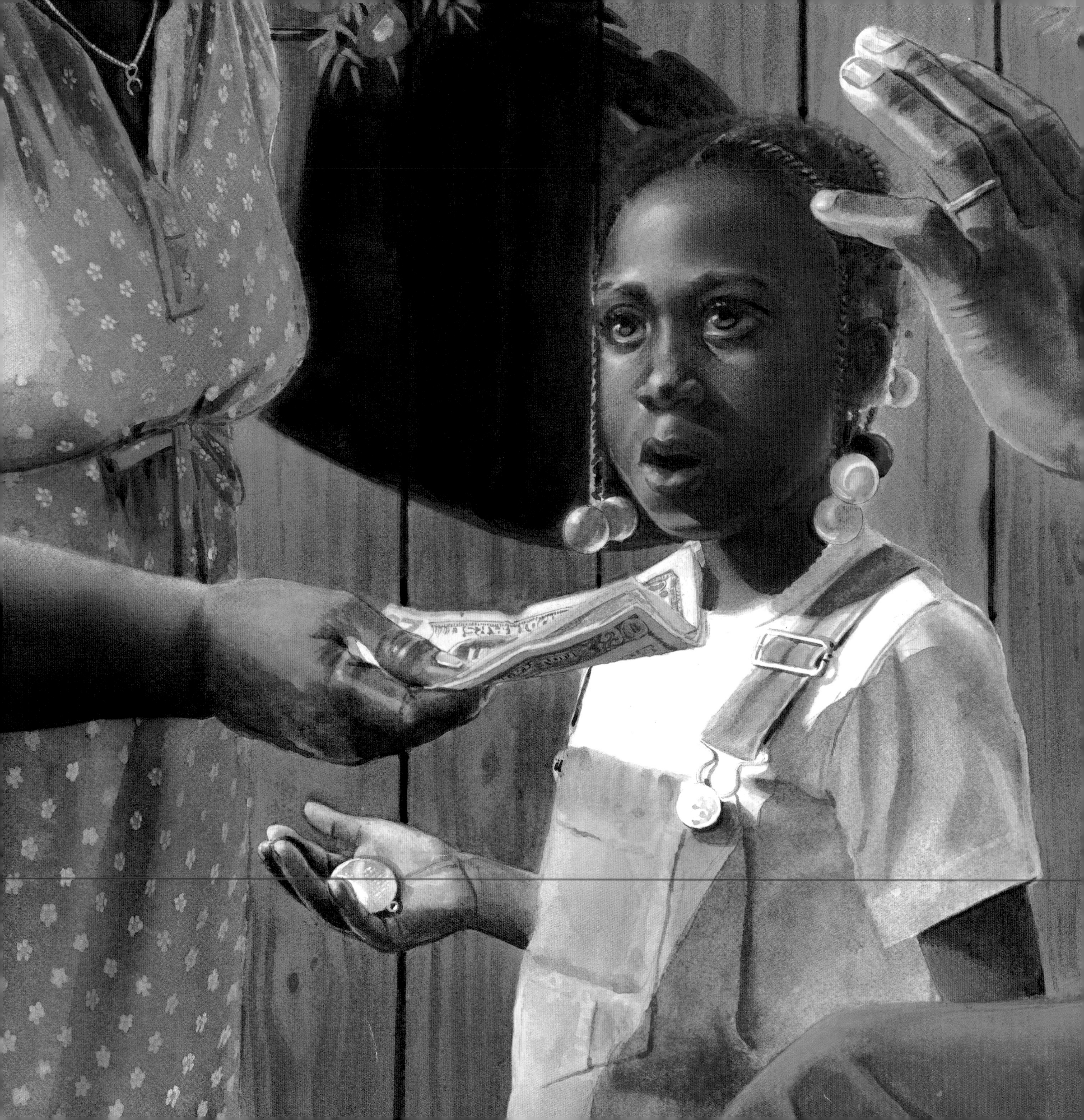

And forgive us our debts
as we forgive our debtors.

And lead us not into temptation,
but deliver us from evil.

For yours
is the kingdom,
and the power,
and the glory

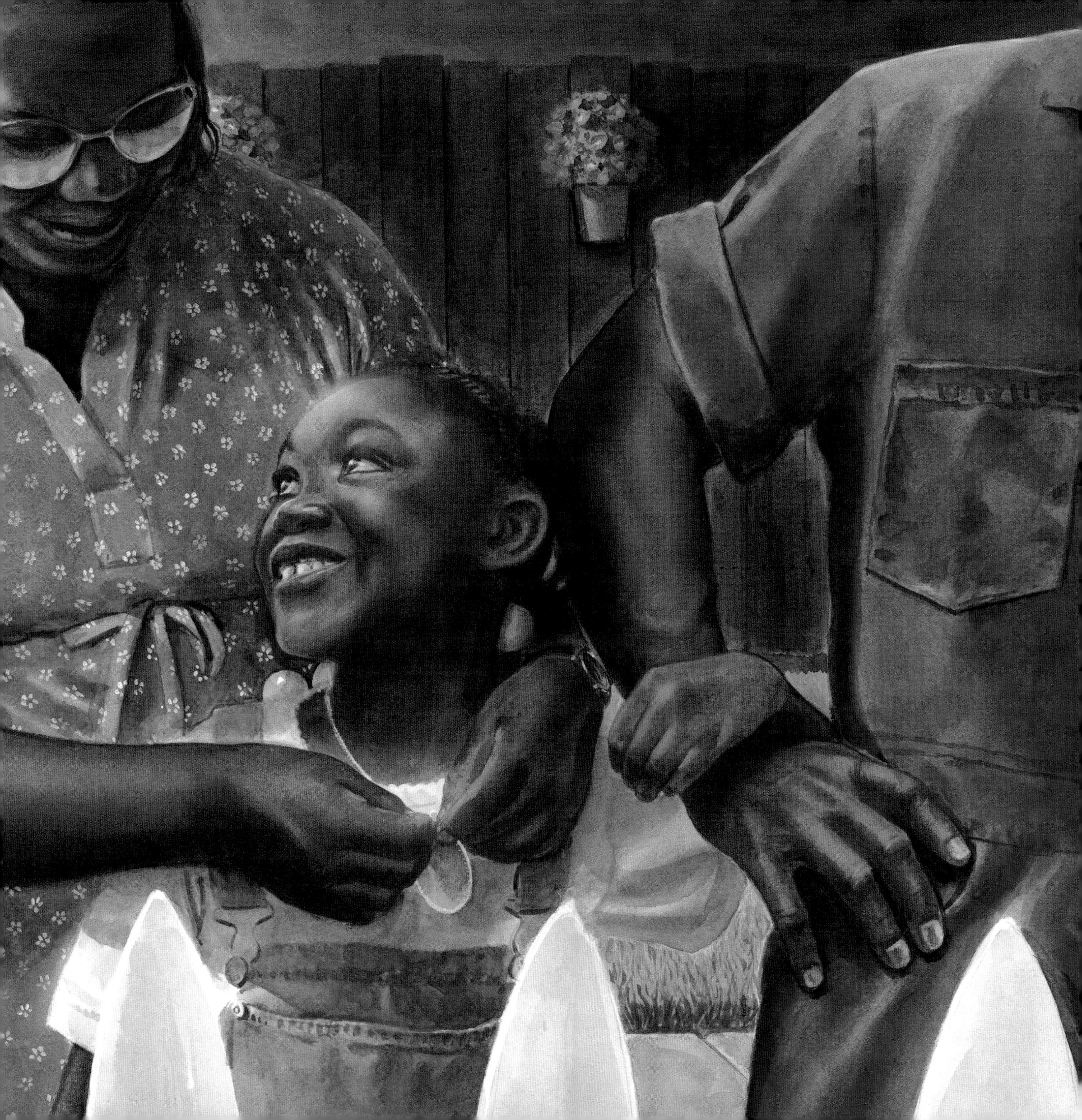

forever.

Our Father in heaven,
hollowed be your name.
Your kingdom come.
Your will be done
on earth as it is in heaven.
Give us this day our daily bread.
And forgive us our debts,
as we forgive our debtors.
And lead us not into temptation,
but deliver us from evil.
For yours is the kingdom,
and the power,
and the glory forever.
Amen.

Amen.

LTSS Lineberger Memorial Library
3 5898 00111 7858